Canoe and Camp Cookery

Seneca

Canoe and Camp Cookery

The present edition is a reproduction of previous publication of this classic work. Minor typographical errors may have been corrected without note; however, for an authentic reading experience the spelling, punctuation, and capitalization have been retained from the original text.

ISBN: 979-8-88830-325-2

CONTENTS

CHAPTER IV

CHAPTER V

CHAPTER VI

PART II—CAMP COOKERY

CHAPTER I

CHAPTER II

CHAPTER III

CHAPTER IV

CHAPTER V

CHAPTER VI

CHAPTER VII

PREFACE

A book in the writer's possession, entitled "Camp Cookery," contains the following recipe:

"Boiled Green Corn.—Boil twenty-five minutes, if very young and tender. As it grows older it requires a longer time. Send to the table in a napkin."

The writer of the above is a good housewife. She cannot conceive that anybody will attempt to boil green corn who does not know such rudiments of the culinary art as the proper quantity of water to put into the pot and the necessity of its being slightly salted and at a boil when the corn is put in, instead of fresh and cold; and, like the careful cook that she is, she tells the camper to send the ears to the camp "table" in a "napkin."

The faults of the above recipe are the faults of all recipes furnished by the majority of books on out-door life. They do not instruct in those rudimentary principles of cooking so important to the outer who has eaten all his life no food except that furnished him ready for instant despatch; and they commend to the camper dishes that require materials and utensils for their preparation which are seldom at hand in the field and forest.

The object of this little volume is to give to the Corinthian cruiser and the camper some practical recipes for simple but substantial dishes, in such a manner that the veriest novice in the art of the kitchen may prepare palatable food with no more materials and paraphernalia than are consistent with light cruising and comfortable camping. The first part, "Canoe Cookery," instructs in such dishes as the limited outfit of the canoeist or camper who "packs" his dunnage afoot will admit of, while the second part, "Camp Cookery," deals with the more elaborate menu that can be prepared when ease of transportation will allow the carriage of a more extensive supply.

Few of the recipes given are original with the compiler. Some have been obtained from trappers and hunters, others from army and navy cooks, and a few from cook books; but all have been practically tested in camp or on a cruise by the writer, whose pleasure in out-door cooking is only equalled by his delight in out-door life.

PART I

CANOE COOKERY

CHAPTER I

Outfit for Cooking on a Cruise.—Value of a Single Receptacle for Everything Necessary to Prepare a Meal.—The Canoeist's "Grub Box."—The Same as a Seat.—Water-tight Tins.—Necessary Provisions and Utensils.—Waterproof Bags for Surplus Provisions.— Portable Oven.—Canoe Stoves.—Folding Stoves a Nuisance.—Hints for Provisioning for a Cruise.

For canoe cruising a certain amount of food supplies and the necessary utensils for cooking should be carried in a single box or chest, so that when one cooks a meal on board he may have in one receptacle everything necessary for preparing a meal, and when going ashore for his repast he can take in his hands everything requisite at one journey. If on a long cruise the large portion of his food supply may be kept in different parts of the canoe, but the box should contain sufficient for at least three meals, and can be replenished from the larger store when stopping for the night or at a camping place for any length of time. The larger the box that his stowage room will allow the greater will be the comfort of the canoeist.

The box may be made of wood, tin or galvanized iron. The

1

former costs but little, can be made by the cruiser himself, and if properly made and properly taken care of, should answer the purpose; but a box of either japanned or painted tin or galvanized iron will stand much knocking about without fracture, and is therefore preferable when its expense is no objection.

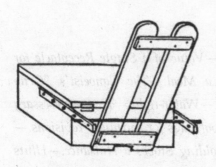

Of course it must be water-tight, and if made of wood the nicest joining and dove-tailing must be done, and it should be varnished inside and out with shellac or boat varnish. Arbitrary dimensions cannot be given because of the varying sizes of canoes and the different amounts of provisions carried on cruises, therefore let each canoeist first determine what amount and variety of eatables he will carry, and then construct the box according to his needs and his stowage room in the cockpit. If made of wood quarter inch or 5/16 stuff (pine) will do, and if the box is to be used as a seat the top and bottom pieces should be heavier, say 3/8 of an inch. The cover should be two inches deep and the handle by which the box is carried should be a thin, wide, flat strap tacked to the cover. If the box is not used as a seat but is stowed under the deck it will be found an advantage to have the flanges of the cover fall over the side pieces of the box and the strap tacked to one end piece, carried over the cover and fastened by a hook to an eye in the other end piece in reach of the hand, so that the cover may be removed and articles obtained from the box without taking it from under the deck. If used as a seat the cover

2

may be hinged on one side and two hooks fastened at the ends on the other, and for the back rest two pieces of three-quarter inch pine are screwed to the sides, running aft horizontally six or eight inches from the aftermost end of the box, holes being bored in them an inch apart "athwartship" and cut opposite each other, through which a quarter-inch brass rod is passed for the back rest to play on. As the lower end of the back rest strikes the end of the box near the floor when in use, it may be "slanted" as inclination demands by changing the brass rod from one set of holes to another.

To carry the provisions in the box so that they will not mix or spill, several water-tight tins should be used. The Consolidated Fruit Jar Company, 49 Warren Street, New York, makes tin screw-tops for jars and canisters that are perfectly water-tight. Send for several of these tops, of assorted sizes, and have a tinsmith make the tin cans of the dimensions you desire, so that they will nest in the box closely. The same company will also furnish you with a pint or quart earthen jar with water-tight screw-top, in which butter may be kept sweet for a long time in hot weather, and which may be enveloped in a net and lowered to the bottom of the river or lake without fear of its leaking.

In the tin cans may be carried coffee, tea (or cocoa), sugar, flour (or meal), rice and alcohol. (A special screw-top is made for fluid cans.) Pepper and salt are in small spice boxes with two covers, the one underneath being perforated. Eggs are safest carried in the tins with the flour, coffee and rice; bread and bacon (or salt pork) are wrapped in macintosh and put near the top of the chest; the vinegar goes in a whisky flask (mark it to avoid

3

mistakes), and canned goods, condensed milk, baking powder, etc., in their own cans. The alcohol stove and utensils necessary to cook a meal should go in the box, such as coffee pot, cup, fork, knife, spoon, frying pan and plates. The coffee pot should be of small size, with handle and lip riveted. If soldered, they are likely to melt off. Cups or plates should be of tin or granite ware. The fork and knife have their sheaths of leather inside the box cover. The plates should nest in the frying pan, which should have no handle, and is fastened inside the chest cover by two buttons, so that it may be readily released. Next the knife and fork have a sheath for a pair of small blacksmith's pliers. This instrument serves as a handle to the frying pan and a lifter for everything on the fire, and can always be kept cool. A three-quart tin or granite ware pail is necessary for stews, and two smaller ones may be nested in it, of two-quart and three-pint capacity, respectively. Put the can of condensed milk in the smallest pail. It will be out of the way, and won't make the rest of the things in the chest sticky. If you carry potatoes, onions or other vegetables, always have enough in the chest for three meals. The surplus supplies of provisions, such as vegetables, extra bread, crackers, flour, meal, pork or bacon, etc., should be carried in waterproof bags, and they can then be stowed wherever necessary to properly trim the canoe. These waterproof bags may be used also for clothing and blankets. They are made of unbleached muslin, sewn in a lap seam, with a double row of stitches. When sewn they are dipped in water and slightly shaken to remove the drops, and then while wet a mixture of equal parts of boiled oil, raw oil and turpentine is applied to the outside with a brush. This takes about a week to become thoroughly dry, and then another coat is put on without

4

dampening the cloth, and if a little liquid drier is added to the mixture, this coat will dry in four or five days. Having prepared several bags, the provisions, clothing, blankets, etc., are put in the bag, and its mouth is inserted in that of another bag of the same size, the latter being drawn on like a stocking as far as it will go. If several bags are used instead of one or two large ones, the canoe can be trimmed and packed to better advantage.

A canoeist's portable oven is made of two small basins, one of which has "ears" riveted to its rim, so that when it is placed bottom up on the other the ears will spring over the rim of the second basin, thus making an oven that is not air-tight, allowing gases to escape. The basins should be made of sheet-iron, and, as their interiors can easily be kept clean, they answer very well for soup dishes. Instructions for baking in them will be given later on. These should not go in the provision chest, as they will smut everything with which they come in contact. Butter, I have found, keeps better in its jar outside of the chest than in. Outside, too, are kept a small jug of molasses, and a jug of fresh water, if cruising on the "briny."

There is no perfect canoe stove. The "flamme forcé" is probably as good as any. It takes up a little more room than the folding "pocket" variety, and it does not give more heat; but it burns for a longer time, and is not top-heavy when a heavy pot or pan is set on it. For cooking in large utensils have three of these flamme forcé alcohol lamps, light them and place them side by side, and you can cook in this way a dozen slapjacks at once on a big griddle, if you like. Danforth, the fluid man, makes a small canoe stove that would be preferable to all others if his fluid were obtainable at all the corners of the earth that canoeists frequent;

5

but unfortunately it is not. Beware of "folding stoves" to use ashore and burn wood in. They are the greatest possible nuisances—smutty, red-hot and cumbersome. Don't carry an oil stove. But if you really must, put the nasty thing in a large bucket, and only remove it from this receptacle when absolutely necessary.

Now as to eatables in general, besides what I have already mentioned, condensed milk is a good thing, but condensed coffee, condensed eggs and condensed beef are abominations. Self-raising or Hecker's prepared flour, wheat, rye, Indian or Graham, is easily made into bread and slapjacks. The directions come with the packages. Pilot bread will keep an indefinite time, and is not so unpalatable as hard-tack. Indian meal is very nutritious and easily made up, as it requires nothing to lighten it; scald it before using when it is not fresh. Canned tomatoes, corn, fruits, beans, soups, salmon, etc., are easy to prepare, and can be stored as ballast in the canoe. Mr. Hicks, of the Toronto Canoe Club, prepares certain kinds of food in cans for ballast as follows, according to the American Canoeist:

"Get a number of flat square tin cans made like oyster cans, of a handy size to lie under your floor boards. Then cook a turkey, some chickens, a sirloin of beef, etc. Cut the hot meat up into large dice-shaped pieces, and put it in the tins hot, then pour melted fat in till the tins are full, and then solder them tight. Get as much meat in as you can before putting in the fat. Put up fruit in square flat cans in the same way. There is your ballast, and heavy stuff it is. When the provisions run short let the crew feed on the ballast. The preparation described is far more nutritious

6

than canned corned beef, is more palatable, and will keep indefinitely—that is, throughout a very long cruise."

I have not tried this method of preserving provisions, but the theory is excellent, and I do not see why it would not be a feasible scheme. The Brunswick canned soups are the cheapest made, are easily prepared and as wholesome as any; but I have known squeamish canoeists who would not use them because they didn't like the looks of the powder to which they are desiccated. Dried beef, corned beef, lemons and sardines make good additions to an outfit. Potatoes, onions and other vegetables should be procured en route as needed, if possible.

As it may puzzle some neophytes to know how much of each article of food to take on a cruise, I give below the exact amount of provisions I carried on a cruise of a week last autumn. I did not run short of anything at the end of the week, but I had not provisions enough left for three square meals: 1 lb. sugar (cut loaf); 1/8 lb. tea; 1 lb. flour; 1-1/2 lbs. crackers; 1/2 lb. lard; 1/2 lb. rice; 1/2 lb. bacon; 3/4 lb. coffee; 1 lb. butter; 1 can condensed milk; 3 loaves bread; 3/4 peck potatoes; 1/2 peck meal; 1 pint molasses; 2 oz. pepper; 1 bottle pickles; 1 bottle yeast powder; 1 qt. salt.

CHAPTER II

Canoeists will hardly take the time and trouble to make soups out of meats and vegetables, unless they are in a permanent camping place for some length of time. Nearly all soups require several hours to cook properly, as they must be boiled very slowly to retain the aroma of the ingredients used.

Canned soups, therefore, are the handiest for the canoeist or single-hand cruiser. I can recommend the Brunswick variety as cheap, convenient, wholesome and easy to prepare if the directions on the cans are implicitly followed. Any variation from these instructions, however, is certain to result in an unpalatable mess. The higher priced soups, Huckins' and other varieties, are more like home-made soups than the Brunswick kind, and hence a fastidious taste will prefer them. They are bulkier to carry, but are quite as easily prepared, and I would recommend those made by Huckins as especially good. The great objection to them is their high price.

There are a few good soups that can be prepared from materials readily accessible to the canoeist, and in a comparatively short time. These are:

8

Oyster Soup

Put a quart of milk and a piece of butter as large as an egg into the pot and heat gradually. When hot, stir in the strained liquor of one pint of oysters, very gradually, to prevent the milk from curdling, then one-quarter pound of crushed crackers or bread crumbs. When it has come to a boil put in the oysters (one pint), and let it cook till the edges of the oysters curl up, when it should be seasoned and served.

Clam Soup

Exactly the same as oyster soup, using clams instead of oysters.

Onion Soup

Put three tablespoonfuls of butter in a frying pan, cut six large onions in slices, and stir them into the butter over the fire till they begin to cook. Then cover tight and set them where they will simmer slowly for half an hour. Put a quart of milk with a tablespoonful of butter on to boil, and while this is doing stir into the onions a tablespoonful of flour while they are simmering. Turn the mixture into the boiling milk and cook quarter of an hour, seasoning with salt and pepper. If an old tin pan is handy that you can use for the purpose, the soup will be improved by knocking small holes in the bottom of the pan, thus making a colander, and straining the soup through it, afterwards adding the well-beaten yolks of four eggs and cooking three minutes longer.

Tomato Soup

Mix one tablespoonful of flour and a piece of butter the size of an egg into a smooth paste, and if you have onions, chop up fine one medium-sized one. Prepare about one pound of tomatoes by scalding, peeling and slicing them (the same amount of canned tomatoes may be used), and put all the ingredients with a pinch of salt into one pint of cold water. Boil gently for an hour, stirring frequently enough to dissolve the tomatoes and prevent burning, then stir in one cup of boiled milk, and let it come again to a boil, constantly stirring. Season and serve. The soup will be good if the milk is omitted.

CHAPTER III

Fish.—Fish Caught in Muddy Streams.—Kill your Fish as Soon as Caught.—Fish Grubs.—Fish Fried, Planked, Skewered, and Boiled.— Fish Sauce, Fish Roe, Shell-Fish.

Fish should naturally have a prominent place in the canoeist's larder. Few streams that he will navigate are entirely destitute of edible fish, and a few minutes spent in angling will amply repay the cruiser.

Fish caught out of muddy streams have an unpleasant taste, and their flavor can be improved by soaking them half an hour or more in strong salted water. Fish should be killed as soon as caught by a sharp rap on the back just aft of the head with a stick or the handle of your big knife, not only in justice to the fish, but because he tastes better, for the same reason that a butchered steer is preferable to one smothered to death.

You may find grubs in fish along the backbone in July and August. You will generally remove them by taking out the backbone and its branches. But if you don't get them all out, never mind; they are good to eat; but if any one of the party is squeamish, tell him you have got them all out anyway: he won't know any better after they are cooked. It is supposed that everybody has known how to clean fish ever since he was a schoolboy, so we will proceed at once to the instructions for cooking.

11

Fried Fish

Small fish may be fried whole, but large ones should be cut up. Have enough pork fat or lard bubbling hot in the frying-pan to well cover the fish. Smear the fish well with dry corn meal or flour, or, what is better, dip it into well-beaten egg and then into bread or cracker crumbs, and fry both sides to a clear golden brown. Sprinkle lightly with pepper and salt just as it is turning brown.

Planked Fish

Shad, flounders, sunfish or any other "flat" fish may be "planked." Cut off the head and tail, split open the back, but do not cut clear through the belly, leaving the fish so that it may be opened wide like a book and tacked on a plank or piece of bark. Tack some thin slices of bacon or pork to the end of the fish that will be uppermost when before the fire, and, if you like, a few slices of raw onion sprinkled with pepper and salt. Sharpen one end of the plank and drive it into the ground, before a bed of hot coals. Catch the drippings in a tin cup or large spoon and baste the fish continually till it smells so good you can't wait another instant to eat it. It is then done.

12

Skewered Trout

Sharpen a small, straight stick, and on it skewer small trout and thin slices of bacon or pork in alternation. Hold over a bed of hot coals and keep constantly turning, so that the juices will not be lost in the fire. A very few minutes will suffice to cook the trout.

Boiled Fish

Tie or pin the fish (which should not weigh less than three pounds) in a clean cloth. If the pot is too small for the fish, skewer the tail into the mouth. Put into enough boiling water to cover it about an inch, and simmer steadily until done. Some fish boil quicker than others; as a general rule those of white flesh requiring less time than those of a darker tinge. If a couple of tablespoonfuls of salt and four ditto of vinegar are put into the water the fish will cook sooner. About twenty-five minutes are necessary for a three-pound fish, and over that six minutes extra to every pound. An underdone fish is not fit to eat, and one boiled too long is insipid. When the meat separates easily from the backbone it is cooked just right. Take it up, remove the cloth carefully, and pour over it the following hot

Fish Sauce

Put two tablespoonfuls of butter and two ditto of flour into a hot frying pan over the fire and mix them together with a spoon into a smooth paste. Pour over very gradually about a pint of the water in which the fish was boiled, stirring it well in. Boil up once and season with pepper and salt. If an acid taste is desired, add a few drops of vinegar.

Boiled Fish Roe

Wash and wipe the roes with a soft cloth. Wrap in a cloth and boil the same as fish. Or, they may be tied inside the fish with a string and boiled with it.

Fried Fish Roe

Prepare as above, dredge in meal or flour, and fry exactly as fish.

Soft Crabs

Have enough boiling hot grease in a pan over a hot fire to cover the crabs. Throw them in as soon as possible after they are taken, with a little salt. Let them brown and turn them once. When done cut off the gills or "dead men's fingers," and serve on toast.

Hard Shell Crabs

These are best steamed. Boil two cups of water in your largest pail. Put in two or three large handfuls of grass and then the crabs, as soon as possible after they are caught. Over them put more grass, and, covering the pail, let them steam thoroughly over the fire for twenty minutes. When done, eat all except the shell, the gills and the stomach, which last is in an easily distinguished sack. Be sure to have sufficient water in the pail to keep up the steam for the requisite time.

Fried Oysters

Strain the liquor from the oysters. Crush crackers into fine crumbs; or, if you have no crackers, toast some slices of bread and crush them fine. Beat up an egg (both white and yolk) in a tin cup with a spoon. Dip the oysters into the beaten egg, then roll them in the crumbs, and put over the fire in a pan of boiling fat over half an inch deep. Turn when brown on one side, and let the other side brown. If the oysters are small do not prepare them singly, but place them two together (the large portions at opposite ends), then immerse them in the egg and crumbs together. If the crumbs do not readily adhere, pat the oysters gently while rolling them in the crumbs.

Blanketed Oysters

Get the largest oysters you can find, cut fat bacon into very thin slices, wrap an oyster in each slice, and skewer with a small stick. Heat a frying pan very hot, put in your oysters, and cook long enough to just crisp the bacon—not over two minutes— taking care that they do not burn. Serve immediately without removing the skewers.

CHAPTER IV

Meats and Game.—Salt Pork.—Ham and Eggs.—Broiling and Boiling Meats.—Pigeons, Squirrels, Ducks, Grouse, Woodcock, Rabbits, Frogs, etc.

In selecting salt pork pick out that which is smooth and dry. Damp, clammy pork is unwholesome. Canned corn beef is palatable, and useful in making hash, but is sometimes poisonous from the solder used in sealing the cans. If canned beef is carried, use only the portion that does not touch the metal of the cans, throwing away the remainder.

Fried Salt Pork (or Bacon)

Slice thin, put in frying pan with cold water enough to cover, let it come to a boil and boil two or three minutes; then turn off the water and fry brown on both sides; or, soak one hour in cold water, then roll in bread or cracker crumbs and fry with a little butter or lard in the pan.

Broiled Salt Pork

Slice thin, and broil on the end of a green switch held over the coals, using extra care that the smoke and flame from the drippings do not reach the pork.

Ham and Eggs

Fry the ham first, the same as pork or bacon, and fry the eggs in the fat left in the pan. Break each egg separately into a cup, and thence transfer it to the pan, by which means the yolks are kept intact and bad eggs are discovered before it is too late. While the eggs are frying dip up some of the fat with a spoon and pour it over the tops of the eggs.

Broiled Steaks

If the steak is tough, beat it on both sides, but not enough to tear the meat and allow the juices to escape. Sharpen a green switch at the end, secure the steak on it, and place over a bed of hot coals, turning frequently. Do not let the escaping juices set fire to the meat. Season, after it is done, with pepper and salt, and if a gravy is desired, put a half teaspoonful of salt, half as much pepper, and a piece of butter or fat as large as a duck's egg into a hot dish, and add two tablespoonfuls of boiling water. Pour it over the steak slowly, so that every part of the latter will be moistened.

Broiling in a Frying Pan

Broiling can be done as well with a frying pan as with a gridiron, and all the juices are preserved. Heat the empty pan very hot first, then put in the meat to be broiled, cover over with a tin plate, and turn the meat often in the pan.

Boiled Meat

Put the meat into enough boiling water so that the former will be a little more than covered. Cover the pot and boil till cooked, which will take about fifteen minutes for every pound of meat. Skim constantly while boiling, and turn the meat several times. Replenish when necessary with boiling water. One teaspoonful of salt for each five pounds of meat should be put into the pot a short time before the meat is done. If there is a layer of fat on top after the meat is cold, remove it. Beef or venison may be used for frying.

Fried Pigeons

Dress them, parboil until they are tender, then cut off the legs and wings, slice off the breast pieces, roll in flour or meal and fry in hot pork fat till they are nicely browned. Grouse, ducks, quail, snipe and plover may also be fried, but are better cooked as given below. Snipe, quail and plover need no parboiling.

Fried Squirrels

Skin and clean, cutting off heads, tails and feet. Parboil and fry, same as pigeons.

Roast Quail, Snipe or Plover

Dress and impale each on a stick with a piece of fat pork in each bird. Set the stick in the ground before a big bed of live coals in a slanting position so that the heat will fall evenly on all portions of the bird, and turn frequently till a sharp sliver will easily pass through the breast. Catch the drippings in a tin cup and pour over the birds again and again, and if they are served on toast pour the drippings also on the toast. The blacksmith's pliers mentioned in Chapter I. will come in handy for turning the birds before the fire on their sticks and holding the cup to catch the drippings. Without this tool the cook's hands are likely to be roasted by the time the birds are done.

Roast Ducks and Grouse

Parboil till tender, then roast as above.

Roast Woodcock

Pick, but do not clean. Roast as above without parboiling. Remove the entrails after the bird is done.

Rabbits or Hares

These require considerable parboiling unless young. They may be fried like squirrels, cutting them into pieces, or made into stews.

Stewed Rabbit

After skinning and cleaning the rabbit cut it into pieces, and wash again in cold water. Mince an onion, cleanse and cut into small pieces one-half pound of fat salt pork, and put with the cut-up rabbit into a pot with about a pint of cold water. Season with pepper and salt, cover the pot and let it simmer till the flesh can be easily pierced with a sharp sliver. Take it up when done and set where it will keep warm, and make a gravy by adding to the water left in the pot one cup of boiling milk or water, stirring in gradually one well-beaten egg and one or two tablespoonfuls of flour made into a smooth paste with cold water. Boil one minute and then pour over the rabbit. This gravy will be nearly or quite as good if the egg is omitted.

Stewed Ducks or Pigeons

Stew exactly the same as rabbits. The pork may be omitted without detracting from the edible quality of the dish.

Frogs

Use only the hind legs of small frogs, but both the fore and hind legs of large ones. They are best broiled, but may be fried in butter.

CHAPTER V

Vegetables.—Potatoes and Green Corn, Boiled, Fried, Roasted and Stewed.

The canoeist, whose stowage room is limited, will not carry with him a variety of vegetables, therefore completer directions for cooking these edibles will be left for Part II. of this book, and instructions will here be given only for the preparation of the potatoes, which he will most certainly carry, and green corn, which, in its season, he can obtain readily, if his cruise leads him through a farming country. These two articles will form the canoeist's mainstay in the vegetable line, and can be prepared in several appetizing ways.

Boiled Potatoes

Small or medium-sized potatoes are preferable to large ones. Choose those with small eyes, as those with large eyes are generally about to sprout and are of poor quality. Do not pare unless they are very old, and in the latter case put them in cold water and allow it to boil. If they are of unequal size cut the large ones, so that they will boil evenly; wash, cut out bad places and eyes, and slice off a piece of skin at each pointed end. Put, unless

24

old, into enough boiling salted water to cover them, and simmer steadily till a sliver will easily pierce the largest. Strain when done, and set the pot near the fire, shaking them occasionally to dry them.

Mashed Potatoes

After boiling, peel and mash thoroughly with the bottom of a large bottle, working in pepper, salt, butter, and sufficient hot milk or water to make them into the consistency of soft dough. If mashed in an iron pot they will be discolored, but will taste just as good as if mashed in tin or earthenware.

Roasted Potatoes

Wash and wipe them dry, and cut off the ends. Bury them in the ashes till a sliver will easily pierce them. Do not make the common mistake of putting them among the live coals of the fire, or they will be burned, not cooked through.

Fried Cooked Potatoes

Peel and slice cold cooked potatoes, and put them into enough "screeching hot" lard or pork fat to cover the bottom of the pan. Stir frequently and fry slowly, seasoning with pepper and salt.

Fried Raw Potatoes

Wash, peel, and slice very thin. Put few at a time into enough boiling fat to float the slices. If too many are put in at one time they will chill the fat and will not fry evenly. Turn and fry a light brown on both sides. When done remove with a fork, leaving as much grease as possible, and shake them up in a covered dish to eliminate the grease still further.

Stewed Potatoes

Cut cold boiled potatoes into pieces the size of a hickory nut, put them into enough boiling milk to cover them, and let them simmer slowly till the milk is nearly exhausted, stirring frequently to prevent burning. Season with pepper, salt and butter.

Sweet Potatoes

Are cooked the same as Irish potatoes, but require longer time.
See time table in Part II.

Boiled Green Corn

The sweetness of corn is better preserved in the boiling if the
outer layer of husks only is stripped off. Turn back the inner
husks and strip off the silk, then replace the inner husks and tie
the ends. Put the corn into enough boiling salt water to cover it.
Boil, if young, twenty-five minutes; if old, nearly or quite twice
as long. After half an hour's boiling, an ear had best be removed
occasionally and the kernels prodded with a sliver, to see if they
have cooked tender. Overboiling spoils corn. Drain off the water
as soon as they are done.

Fried Corn

Cut cold boiled corn from the cob, mix with mashed potatoes,
and fry in butter or pork fat.

27

Roasted Corn

Leave the ear in the husks, cover it well with the hot ashes, and let it remain from forty-five minutes to an hour.

Stewed Corn

Cut the corn from the cob, put it into a pot, barely covering it with cold milk. Season it with pepper and salt, and if common field corn, with sugar. Cover and stew gently till very tender.

CHAPTER VI

Coffee and Tea.—Mush, Johnnycake and Hoecake.—Slapjacks, Corn Dodgers, Ash Cakes, Biscuits, Camp Bread.—Eggs.

Coffee

The simplest way to make good coffee is to put into the pot two tablespoonfuls of the ground and browned berry to each cupful of the beverage. Pour on cold water to the required amount, remove it from the fire when it first boils up, let it stand a few moments in a warm place, and then pour into the pot half a cup of cold water to settle it.

Coffee, No. 2

If the ground coffee is running low or the cook wishes to economize and has plenty of time and utensils, I will give him a recipe which requires much less of the berry to produce the required strength, as follows: Put the dry coffee into the pot, and heat it, stirring it constantly. Then pour over it one quart of boiling water to every two tablespoonfuls of coffee, and set the

29

pot where it will keep hot but not boil. After standing ten or fifteen minutes it is ready to drink.

Tea

For most teas the right proportion is one tablespoonful of tea for every teacup that is to be drawn and one "for the pot." The simplest method of making it is to put cold water on the tea in the pot, set over the fire and let it almost boil. Just as it begins to steam remove it to a place less hot, where it will simmer and not boil for five minutes. If it boils or simmers too long the tannin will be dissolved, and the tea will have a disagreeable astringent taste. When the liquid is all used out of the pot I do not throw away the "grounds," but add one-half the quantity for the next drawing, and so on till the pot is one-third full of grounds, when it is all emptied and the pot thoroughly washed.

Cornmeal Mush

The main difficulties in making good cornmeal mush are the care necessary to prevent the formation of lumps and the long time required to cook it. The surest way to avoid lumps is to mix the meal first with cold water enough to make a thin batter, and then pour this batter into the pot of boiling water (slightly salted) very gradually, so as not to stop the boiling process. Sufficient of the batter should be stirred in to make a thin mush, and the latter should then be boiled until it is of such consistency that it will hang well together when taken out with a spoon. The longer it is allowed to boil the better it will be, and if long boiling makes it too thick, add more boiling water. It can be advantageously boiled two hours, but is eatable after twenty minutes' boil. If it is sprinkled into the pot of boiling water dry, do so very gradually and stir it constantly to prevent its lumping.

Fried Cold Mush

Cut cold cornmeal mush into slices half an inch thick, and fry on both sides in boiling pork fat or butter. Or, dip each slice into beaten egg (salted), then into bread or cracker crumbs, and fry. If fried in lard add a little salt.

Oatmeal Mush

Is made the same as cornmeal mush, but must always be sprinkled dry into the pot of boiling water.

31

Johnnycake

Make a thick batter by mixing warm (not scalding) water or milk with one pint of cornmeal, and mix in with this a small teaspoonful of salt and a tablespoonful of melted lard. Grease your bake-tins (described in Chapter I.) thoroughly with lard or butter, set the Johnnycake batter in one, cover over with the other, and bury the oven amongst the hot coals and ashes of the camp-fire, heaping the coals around it so as to have an equal heat on all portions of the oven. In twenty minutes dig out the oven, open it with the pliers and test the Johnnycake. It should be thoroughly baked in a good fire in from twenty to thirty minutes. If the meal is mixed with scalding water it will be lumpy and difficult to work into a batter.

Hoe Cakes

Johnnycake batter, thinned down with more warm water or milk, may be fried the same as slapjacks.

Slapjacks

To properly cook slapjacks the frying pan should be perfectly clean and smooth inside. If it is not, too much grease is required in cooking. Scrape it after each panful is cooked, and then only occasional greasing will be required, and this is best done with a clean rag containing butter. Drop thin batter in with a spoon, so that the cake will be very thin. Disturb it as little as possible, and when the cake is cooked firm on one side, turn it and cook on the other.

Cornmeal Slapjacks

One quart of cold water is mixed with meal enough to make a thin batter, one teaspoonful of salt and one or two teaspoonfuls of baking powder having been stirred into the latter. The addition of one or two well-beaten eggs will improve it. Cook on a very hot pan, as above.

Wheat Slapjacks

Make as above, except using wheat flour, and adding last of all

33

one heaping tablespoonful of melted lard or butter, thoroughly stirred in.

Hecker's Flour Slapjacks

Mix well one pint of Hecker's prepared flour with one-half pint of cold milk or water. Cook as above.

Corn Dodgers

Mix one pint of corn meal, one small teaspoonful of salt and one tablespoonful of sugar with warm (not scalding) water enough to make a moderately stiff batter. Make into flat cakes about three-quarters of an inch thick, and fry in boiling fat till brown. Fried in bacon fat and eaten with the fried bacon they are very palatable.

Corn Pone or Ash Cakes

If unprovided with the portable oven or bake tin recommended

34

in Chapter I., mix up a pint of corn meal with water and a pinch of salt into a stiff dough, make into cakes, and set them on a clean, hot stone close to the coals of a hot fire. When the outside of the cakes has hardened a little cover them completely in hot ashes. In fifteen to twenty-five minutes rake them out, brush off the ashes, and devour quickly. Any ashes adhering after the brushing process can be readily removed by cutting out the irregularities in the crust where they have lodged. The writer has known a party of ladies, who could scarcely be induced to taste these cakes at first, become so fond of them after a trial as to insist upon having them three times a day for a week in camp.

Baking Powder Biscuits

Put one pint of flour into a deep vessel, mix into it two large teaspoonfuls of baking powder[1] and a pinch of salt; then rub in one small teaspoonful of lard or butter, lessening the amount of salt if the latter is used, and add enough cold water or milk to make a soft dough. Handle as little as possible, but roll into a sheet about three-quarters of an inch thick, and cut into round cakes with an empty tin cup. Lay the biscuits close together in a well-greased tin, and bake a few minutes in the coals, as described above for Johnnycake.

---

[1] See note on baking powder in the chapter of "Hints."

Hecker's Flour Biscuits

Require only the mixing of the flour with water, and are then ready to bake.

Quick Camp Bread

Make a biscuit dough as above, and roll it to a thickness of half an inch. Grease a frying-pan and set it over the hot embers till the grease begins to melt. Then put the dough into the pan and set it on the fire, shaking it frequently to prevent the dough from adhering. When the crust has formed on the bottom, take the bread out of the pan and prop it up on edge, close to the fire, turning it occasionally to insure its being baked through. Or, turn the bread in the frying pan until it is cooked through. This bread will not keep soft long, and the writer prefers, when depending for any length of time upon his own baking, to make.

Unleavened Bread

This is the kind almost wholly used by coasting vessels, and is cooked as above in a frying-pan, even when there is a galley-

36

stove with a good hot oven on board the vessel. The dough is mixed up with a quart of wheat flour, one teaspoonful of lard, a teaspoonful of salt and sufficient water to make it stiff. It is then beaten or hammered lustily on a board or smooth log until it becomes elastic. When cut up into biscuit it can be baked in the portable oven among the coals. It is called "Maryland Biscuit" along the Potomac and Chesapeake.

Fried and Boiled Eggs

Are so easy to prepare that no instruction is necessary in these familiar methods of cooking them.

Poached Eggs

Into a frying pan nearly full of boiling water containing a teaspoonful of salt slip carefully the eggs one by one, breaking each previously into a cup. Keep them on the surface of the water, if possible, and boil gently three or four minutes, dipping up some of the water with a spoon and pouring it over the tops of the eggs. Serve on toast.

Scrambled Eggs

Break the eggs into a cup to insure their freshness, and throw them into the frying pan with a lump of butter and salt and pepper. Stir over a fire of coals until they are almost hard. Do not break the yolks at first.

PART II

CAMP COOKERY

CHAPTER I

Outfit.—Go Light as Possible.—Carriage of Provisions and Utensils.—Camp Stoves, Ice-boxes and Hair Mattresses.—The Bed of "Browse."—How to make a Cooking Range Out-of-doors.—Building the Fire.—A Useful Tool.—Construction of Coffee Pot and Frying Pan.—Baking in Camp.—Fuel for Camp-fire.—Kerosene and Alcohol Stoves.—Camp Table.—Washing Dishes, etc.

The remarks given on outfit in Chapter I. of Part I. are, many of them, as well adapted to camp as to canoe cookery. The utensils carried for cooking in a permanent camp, and for more than one person, will of course exceed in number those used by the canoeist, but there will be few additional articles really necessary, even with the varied and extensive bill-of-fare that the possibilities of a three weeks' camp in one place suggest. Even if you have teams and lumber-wagons to carry your outfit into the woods it is better to go light as possible. With few things to find places for the camp can be kept neat and ship-shape, and everything will be handy; while the chances are that a portion of a large and varied outfit will be wasted. Two friends and myself

39

go regularly into camp for three weeks with no added utensils to those mentioned in the canoe outfit except an iron pot and a Dutch oven, and even these additions are seldom used. A large cooking outfit for a camp can be best packed in a large pack basket, such as is generally used in the Adirondacks and Maine woods; but these receptacles are not waterproof, therefore I would recommend that the eatables themselves be carried in waterproofed muslin bags, each variety having its own bag. All together may then be packed in basket, chest or knapsack, as desired. Butter will keep sweet longer in an earthen jar with water-tight cover, as described on page 11, than in any other receptacle I know of. It can be enveloped in a net and lowered to the bottom of a lake or river, or set in a cold spring, or tucked away in the coolest corner of a little cellar dug into a side hill and lined with clean birch bark. If I carry a dozen or two of eggs into the woods with me I let them ride in a tin pail along with plenty of corn meal, and seldom find a broken one among them.

A good many campers—and especially lady campers—think it necessary to carry a camp stove; some people go into the woods with an ice-box and a ton of ice; and others bring with them bedsteads and hair mattresses. I do not camp with such people, and I think every true woodsman will agree with me that these deluded persons do not enjoy to the full the pleasure and wholesome exhilaration of real camp life. A bed of spruce or hemlock browse, properly "shingled" and of a good depth, is the cleanest, softest, most fragrant and healthful couch in the world. If I never camped for any other reason, I would go once a year for the express purpose of enjoying for a brief season the delicious odor and natural elastic softness of this best of beds.

I have never felt the need of ice or ice-box in all my camping experience. A cold spring of water keeps my butter sweet, and I never send to town for butchered meat; if I did perhaps I should find a refrigerator useful.

Now as to camp stoves. A camp of lumbermen will find a stove of some sort a time-saving utensil, for but little time can be spared from their work in the woods to prepare meals, and a dinner can be unquestionably got quicker on a stove than with an open fire. But to a party of pleasure outers whose time in camp is not of so great importance, a camp stove is a superfluous piece of furniture. It is unwieldy to carry, smutty to handle, and makes a camp look like a summer kitchen in a back-yard. Every necessary culinary operation can be performed equally well or even better without it, if the camper knows how to properly make a cooking camp-fire.

The fire, in summer, should not be made so close to the tent as to make that sleeping and lounging place too warm, nor should it be made so far away as to tire the cook from running back and forth with the cooking utensils and grub. Two green logs, five or six feet long and eight to twelve inches in diameter, of a nearly even thickness throughout, are laid on a level piece of ground side by side, about a foot apart at one end, and touching at the other, thus forming an elongated V. With a hatchet hew them on their upper sides until the surface is level enough to support pots and pans in safety. Between these logs build your fire. This should not be done carelessly, but methodically and with patience. Begin with only as many dry shavings as you can grasp in your hand. When these are ablaze, add shavings and bits of

41

dry wood of a little larger size, and then those a little larger than the last, and so on, increasing the size of the sticks very gradually and leading the fire by degrees until it covers all the space between the logs.

When the fire is well under way and blazing brightly at all points, pile on it plenty of split sticks, short, and as near a uniform size as possible, and let them all burn to coals before cooking is commenced. If some of the sticks are large and some small, they will not burn evenly, and by the time the larger ones have become coals, the coals of the smaller ones will have become ashes. And if the sticks are round instead of split, they will not catch fire so easily, and will nest so close together as to give insufficient draft. Driftwood will do to start a fire, but it should never be used after the blaze is well going, because it burns to ashes instead of coals. The best coals result from burning hard wood. Never put a cooking utensil on the fire until the smoke and blaze have ceased. When you have a good bed of coals set the coffee pot on near where the logs join, and the frying pan, large pot, etc., where the logs are further apart. If there is much wind, ashes will be blown about to some extent, and it is best to always keep the open end of the "range" to windward, as the frying pan is generally set on this end, while the coffee pot and other pots being covered, can stand a shower of ashes without harm to their contents. As fast as one dish is cooked, set it on one of the logs where it will keep warm, and use the handy blacksmith's pliers to heap up the live coals under other dishes that are not cooking fast enough.

These pliers can be made by any blacksmith, and should be from twelve to eighteen inches in length, and quite broad in the gripping part, which may with advantage be curved to a slight angle. I always use a frying pan without handle for compactness, and can lift it from any side of the fire with the pliers, which are always cool. I even grip the coffee pot with them and pour the coffee for the whole party without touching it with my hands, saving many a scorch thereby. It is a handy tool in making repairs to boats, and in various other ways proves its value as a necessary part of the camp outfit. The coffee pot should not have a spout, but a lip, riveted on, near its topmost edge. The handle should also be riveted, and should set as near as possible to the top of the pot. A wire bale may be attached for handiness in lifting.

The cooking range above described will suffice for nearly all branches of camp cookery. On it one can fry, broil and boil. When a boil is to be kept up for hours, however, as in cooking beans, greens, and some soups and stews, it will be necessary to set up a forked stake at each end of the fire, hang the kettle on a cross-piece between, and keep up the fire beneath by constant feeding and attention. Do not let the blaze mount so high as to burn or char the cross-piece.

The fire for baking should be made apart from the range. A hole in the ground a little more than deep enough to contain the bake-kettle or Dutch oven should be dug, and of sufficient diameter to allow four or five inches' space on each side of the oven when it is in the hole. Build up a good fire in the hole, and when you have a large quantity of hot coals and ashes, dig out all but a thick layer on the bottom, set in your oven, and pack it all around and on top with the coals and ashes. Cover the whole with a piece of turf or some earth. When baking without an oven, as fish in clay, a bird in its feathers, or a 'possum in its own hide, dig out nearly all the coals, put some green grass or leaves in the bottom, then the fish, bird or beast, then more grass or leaves, then coals and ashes, then earth, and lastly build a small fire on top and keep it burning steadily.

In all the baking recipes recommended in this book a certain time is given for each operation. This time mentioned is only approximate, and it will be found to vary a few minutes, according to the amount of coal used, the kind of firewood, etc. The time necessary to bake a given thing can only be learned exactly by practical experience; but this experience will teach the cook all he needs to know after the first two or three attempts.

In closing my remarks on fires I would suggest that the best wood to be obtained for cooking fires is that from hard wood trees that have fallen in the woods or been cut down, and have lain long enough to become well seasoned. If this is used the fire will stand any ordinary rain, and the camper will not be compelled to resort to his alcohol stove under shelter for any thing short of the equinoctial storm. If wood is damp, a few drops of kerosene, gun oil or alcohol sprinkled on it will be a valuable aid in starting a fire.

I have no love for kerosene stoves. The alcohol "flamme forcé" is more compact, gives a stronger heat (have two, set side by side), and is perfectly clean. If, however, you must take along a kerosene stove, the wind-protected kind manufactured by Adams & Westlake (5 East Fourteenth Street, New York, and 78

Washington Street, Boston) will probably be found the most suitable. Neither the kerosene nor the alcohol stoves should be used when an outdoor fire can be built.

A camp dining-table can be made by driving down four forked stakes in the corners of an imaginary rectangle. Connect the end stakes with cross-pieces, and lay planks from one cross-piece to the other. Make it just high enough to get the legs and feet under comfortably when sitting upon the ground, and build it away from the fire. A camp chest makes a good table, so does a large log with one side hewed level. Each member of a party that I frequently camp with has a tin or wooden box in which fishing tackle, cartridges, tools, etc., are carried. When dinner is prepared a piece of spare canvas is laid upon the grass, the tin dishes and edibles are put upon this, then each man brings his box to the particular corner of the cloth he selects, sits on the grass, crosses his legs, and has each his individual table in his own private box, the cover of which is large enough to hold a tin plate, tin cup, knife and fork, etc.

By all means wash the dishes immediately after each meal. You can smoke your post-prandial pipe and do this at the same time. Have a pot or kettle of water heating while you are eating, and if the frying pan is dirty, fill it with water and let it boil over the coals awhile. Put your dishes into the largest pail, pour hot water over them, tone it down with cold water so you can handle them, and wash the dishes, the least dirty first, with a sponge. Sapolio is good to scour them, but sand is better. Soap is less often used by male campers in dish-washing than it should be. It makes the work much easier. When washed, rinse the tin-ware in cold water, drain and dry with a towel. Wring out the sponge in clean water, and hang it on a bush ready for use again.

Remove all refuse and leavings to a good distance from camp, and never allow the vicinity of the tent to become littered up with tomato cans, old cartridge shells, bones, feathers, corn-husks, etc.

CHAPTER II

Soups. — General Remarks on Cooking Soups. — Soups made of Meat, Vegetables, Deer's Heads, Small Game, Rice, Fish and Turtle.

Soups should be made in camp as often as the materials are at hand. They are wholesome and invigorating, and not difficult to prepare; and so many different kinds can be made that no camper's appetite need be cloyed by lack of variety. Most canned soups are excellent, and the directions for cooking which come with them should be closely followed.

The time given for cooking soups in the recipes that follow may seem unnecessarily long, but if it is done in a less time, it is at a loss in the flavor. Fast boiling drives off considerable of the aroma of the ingredients used, the water evaporates fast and requires constant replenishing with boiling water, which compels the cook to have an additional vessel always on the fire. Constant skimming is necessary, and an occasional slight stirring will prevent any of the vegetables from burning on the pot where but little water is used.

Campers do not commonly have fresh meat in camp, unless in a portion of the country where venison, buffalo or bear meat form a part of the larder. With any one of these, or with beef, we can make what I will call

47

Meat Soup

Use one pound of lean meat (cut into pieces the size of an egg) to a quart of water. Put on the fire with the water cold, and let it heat gradually and simmer rather than boil, skimming it constantly and keeping the cover on the pot when this operation is not being performed. If any cooked meat or bones are to be added, this should be done after the soup has cooked three-quarters of an hour. From four and a half to five hours are necessary for the soup to cook. Just before it is done, season with salt and pepper. If made in an iron pot it should be transferred as soon as done to a tin or earthen vessel. In cold weather this soup may be kept fresh and sweet for a week and "warmed over" as long as it lasts.

Vegetable Soup

Onions, potatoes, carrots, turnips, beets, parsnips, cabbage, cauliflower, pumpkins, squash, etc., should be picked over, washed, pared, and cut into small pieces from a quarter to a half-inch thick, put into a pan of cold water, rinsed and drained. Tomatoes should be scalded, peeled and sliced. Prepare a meat soup as above, and when it has cooked four hours put in all your vegetables except potatoes, which should be put in only about thirty minutes before the soup is done. Stir the soup occasionally

48

to prevent the vegetables from scorching or sticking to the bottom of the pot, and skim frequently. When done take out the vegetables, mash and return them to the soup, boil one minute, season and serve. Canned corn or tomatoes may be used in this soup the same as fresh vegetables.

Deer's Head Soup

Skin the head and split it in pieces, remove the eyes and brains, and wash thoroughly in cold water. Then cook same as meat soup.

Small Game Soup

Squirrels, rabbits, and small game generally can be cleaned and split and made into soup as above. When vegetables are added to soup made of small game, the latter should be removed and strained, and the good meat returned to the pot just before the vegetables are put in, leaving out all the bones, skin, gristle, etc.

Rice Soup

Make a meat soup, with the addition of one sliced onion. Prepare the rice (one-half pound to a gallon of water) by picking it over, washing and draining, and stir it into the soup half an hour before it is done, stirring frequently to prevent burning.

Bean Soup

Pick over two quarts of beans, wash, and soak them over night in cold water. Scrape clean one pound of salt pork, and cut into thin slices. Drain the beans, put them into six quarts of cold water, with one tablespoonful of soda, and let them boil gently for half an hour, skimming constantly. Then drain off all the water and put in the same amount of fresh boiling water. Boil slowly for an hour and a half, stirring frequently; then put in the pork. When the beans have become tender enough to crack, take out the pork and mash the beans into a paste with a wooden masher or the bottom of a large bottle. Then put all back and boil slowly an hour longer. If no soda is used, longer boiling will be necessary. Bean soup will burn if not constantly stirred. Not much salt, but plenty of pepper should be used for seasoning.

Pea Soup

Treat the peas exactly the same as the beans in the above recipe, except as to the preliminary boiling in water with soda. Make the same way as bean soup. Pea soup cools and thickens rapidly, therefore if squares of fried bread are thrown upon the surface before serving, it should be done quickly and while the bread is hot. Use more salt than with the bean soup for seasoning, and boil gently or it will surely burn.

Fish Soup

Cut up large fish, after it has been cooled from a previous cooking, into small pieces, and stew it with a piece of salt pork for two hours.

Turtle Soup

Snapping turtles, "mud turtles" and all tortoises can be made into appetizing soup. Cut their throats to kill them and then let them bleed. Break the shell on the under side, cut out the meat, rejecting the entrails, head and claws, and boil slowly for three hours with some sliced onion.

51

CHAPTER III

Fish.—Fish Baked, Plain and Stuffed.—Fish Gravy.—Fish Chowder.—Clam Chowder.—Orthodox Clam Chowder.

The subject of fish cookery belongs more to the canoeist than to the general camper, for the reason that the former is so constantly among them in their fluid home that he can readily catch a mess, and easily cook them with his small means after he has caught them. That is why nearly all the practical methods of cooking fish are given in Chapter III. of Part I. of this book. There are, however, some ways of preparing fish in camp that the canoeist will hardly attempt, for lack of time or utensils, and these methods will be given here.

Plain Baked Fish

Dig a hole in the ground eighteen inches deep and large enough to contain the fish; build a fire in it and let it burn to coals. Remove the coals, leaving the hot ashes in the bottom, on which place a thick layer of green grass. Put the fish on the grass, cover with another layer of grass; then rake back the coals and loose earth and build a small fire on top. In an hour the baking will be complete, the skin will peel off and leave the flesh clean. A fish

52

prepared this way need not be scaled, but only disembowelled, as the scales will come off with the skin after it is cooked.

Stuffed Baked Fish

Only a large fish should be cooked in this manner, as it is hardly worth the trouble to stuff a small fish. Prepare a stuffing of bread or cracker crumbs, with enough butter or lard to make the mixture moist. Season with pepper and salt, and chop up with it one onion, and a little summer savory or sage, if desired. Clean and wipe the fish dry, put in the stuffing lightly and then sew up the opening. Lay the fish in the bake-kettle or Dutch oven, rub it all over with butter or lard and dredge it with flour, meal or some of the dry crumbs left over from the stuffing. Or, lay thin strips of fat salt pork or bacon on the top. Pour a little boiling water into the bottom to prevent the fish adhering, close the bake-kettle and put it into the fire among the hottest coals. In a very hot oven it should be done in forty minutes. Remove the bake-kettle several times before it is done to baste it. When cooked, serve with the following

Fish Gravy

Put the bake-kettle back on the fire after the fish is removed; stir into the gravy left, gradually, two tablespoonfuls of flour. Let it boil up once, season with pepper and salt, and pour over the fish. If there are squeamish people in camp remove the "black specks" from this gravy with a spoon.

Fish Chowder

Clean the fish and cut up all except the heads and tails into small pieces, leaving out as many bones as possible. Cover the bottom of the pot with slices of fat salt pork; over that a layer of sliced raw potatoes; then a layer of chopped onions; then a layer of fish; on the fish a layer of crackers, first made tender by soaking in water or milk. Repeat the layers, except pork, till the pot is nearly full. Every layer must be seasoned with pepper and salt. Put in enough cold water to moisten the whole mass well, cover the pot closely, set over a gentle fire, and let it simmer an hour or so. Cook it till it is rather thick, then stir it gently, and it is ready to serve. Tomatoes may be added as a layer after the onions.

Clam Chowder

Can be made the same as Fish Chowder, using clams instead of fish, but a large party of sea-beach picnickers will probably prefer the regular

Orthodox Clam Chowder

The first thing necessary is an out-door oven made with flat stones. Start a rousing fire in this and let it burn until every stone is hot all the way through. Then rake out the coals beneath, even to the faintest cinder, so that there will be no smoky taste to the chowder. Then put a couple of stout boughs across the open top of the oven, and cover them with fresh seaweed an inch or two thick. Spread the shelled clams on the seaweed, over them a layer of onions, then a layer of sweet or Irish potatoes, or both, then green corn, then the fish (cleaned and salted and mapped in a cloth, and either a bluefish or a cod, if extra-orthodox), then a lobster, either alive or boiled. Now cover the whole arrangement with a large cloth, and pile on seaweed till no steam escapes. When it has cooked half an hour or so let the company attack it en masse, uncovering it gradually as it is eaten, so as to retain the heat in it as long as possible. The stones should be extremely and thoroughly heated, or the chowder will be a failure, and the cinders should be cleaned out, the chowder put on, and the whole covered with great haste, so as not to give the stones a chance to cool.

56

CHAPTER IV

Meats and Game.—Hash.—Pork and Beans.—Game Stew.—Brunswick Stew.—Roast Venison.—Baked Deer's Head.—Venison Sausages.—Stuffed Roasts of Game.—Woodchucks, Porcupines, 'Possums and Pigs.

Some good recipes for cooking meats and game, which are not given in Part I., are the following:

Frizzled Beef

Cut dried beef into very thin shavings, and put into a frying pan nearly half full of cold water. Set over the fire and let it come to a boil, then stir in a large lump of butter and enough flour to make a good gravy.

Hash

Four pounds of cold boiled meat (not pork) or corned beef, free from bone or gristle, one large parboiled onion, and two pounds of boiled or baked potatoes are chopped and mixed together, seasoned with pepper and salt, and stirred up with about a pint of hot water. Put enough lard or butter into a frying pan to well cover the bottom when melted, and when it is "screeching hot," put in the hash. Stir it for a few minutes, then let it fry till it is brown on the bottom. Corned beef hash requires little salt for seasoning.

Boiled Pork

Soak over night in cold water and put into a pot of cold water over the fire when the boiling begins. Boil same as other meat (see page 19) and save the cake of fat that rises when it is cold for frying purposes. Turnips, cabbage, potatoes and greens are good boiled with the pork. See table for boiling vegetables in the next chapter.

Pork Hash

Cut salt pork or bacon into small dice, and while it is frying over a slow fire cut raw potatoes and onions into thin slices, put them with the pork, cover the frying pan and cook for ten minutes, occasionally stirring.

58

Pork and Beans

The right proportions are two quarts of beans to three pounds of pork. Pick over the beans at night, wash them, and put them to soak in cold water until the next morning. Then if only boiled pork and beans are desired, drain the beans, and put them with the pork in the pot, just cover with cold water, set over the fire (with the cover on the pot), and boil till the beans are tender, skimming the scum off as it rises. If baked beans are wanted parboil the pork and cut it into thin slices, then drain the beans and boil as above. Put half the beans into the bake-kettle, then the pork, then the remainder of the beans, and pour over them half a pint of boiling water. Bake among the coals till the top is crusted brown. If buried in the ground with a good supply of coals it is best to put them in at night when going to bed, and they will be done in the morning. If the bake-kettle is enveloped in hot coals on the surface of the ground they will bake on the outside quicker, but inside, where the pork is, they will not be baked at all. This latter method, therefore, should only be used when in a hurry, and in this case the pork should be scattered around in different portions of the pot, and the beans left may be re-baked for another meal.

Game Stew

Cut up any kind of game, whether furred or feathered, into

small pieces, wash it, and put it in a pot with some pork cut into pieces three inches square, and rather more than enough water to cover it all. Let it boil for half an hour, skimming off the particles that rise to the top. Then add four or five sliced onions, some parsley or summer savory, salt and pepper, and boil slowly for an hour and a half. Half an hour before it is done put in a few pared potatoes, cut to a uniform size.

Brunswick Stew[2]

For a stew for five or six persons the following are the ingredients: two-good-sized or three small squirrels, one quart of tomatoes, peeled and sliced, one pint of butter or lima beans, six potatoes, parboiled and sliced, six ears of green corn cut from the cob, one-half pound of butter, one-half a pound of fat salt pork, one teaspoonful of black pepper, one-half a teaspoonful of cayenne, one gallon of water, one tablespoonful of salt, two tablespoonfuls of white sugar, one onion minced small. Cut the squirrels into joints, and lay in cold water to draw out the blood; put on the gallon of water, with the salt in it, and let it boil for five minutes; put in the onion, beans, corn, pork which has been cut into fine strips, potatoes, pepper and the squirrels; cover closely, and stew two and a-half hours very slowly, stirring the

---

[2] This is a favorite Virginia dish, of which the compiler of this book has eaten, but which he has never cooked. The recipe here given is said by an old Virginian to be reliable.

mass frequently from the bottom to prevent its burning. Then add the tomatoes and sugar, and stew an hour longer. Ten minutes before it is to be taken from the fire, add the butter, cut into bits the size of a walnut, and rolled in flour; give a final boil, taste to see that it is seasoned to your liking, and serve at once.

Flour Gravy

After stews have been taken from the pot stir a tablespoonful of flour gradually into a small quantity of cold water, carefully breaking all the lumps. Then pour this gradually into the boiling liquor left in the pot from the stew, let it boil well two minutes, and serve. If flour is sprinkled dry into boiling water it Will form into lumps at once, no matter how much it is stirred. A tablespoonful of flour will sufficiently thicken nearly a quart of liquor. If what is called "brown gravy" is desired, heat the flour first in a frying pan, stirring it till it is brown.

Roast Venison

The saddle is the best portion for roasting, and after this the shoulder. Hang it by a cord over a huge bed of coals, or use the crotched stakes, impaling the venison on the cross-piece. Insert thin slices of salt pork or bacon in gashes cut with a knife where the flesh is thick enough to admit of "gashing," or skewer them on with hard wood twigs where it is not. Turn frequently. The flesh on the surface will become hard by the time the roast is done, but this can be avoided by covering it with buttered paper fastened on with wooden skewers. From two to three hours are required for roasting.

Baked Deer's Head

Build a fire in a hole in the ground. When it has burned to a good bed of coals put in the deer's head, neck downward, with the skin on but the eyes and brains removed. Cover with green grass or leaves, coals and earth, and build a new fire on top of all. In about six hours exhume the head, remove the skin, and the baking is complete. This method of baking applies as well to the head of any animal.

Forequarter of Venison

This portion is always tough, but may be utilized by stewing it, or making it into

Venison Sausages

Chop up pieces of the forequarter, mix with half as much chopped salt pork, season with pepper and salt, make into balls, and fry.

Stuffed Shoulder of Venison

If you are very "swell" campers-out, and have some port or Madeira wine with you, you may stew the shoulder of venison in the following manner: Extract the bones through the under side and make a stuffing as follows: Chop up suet very fine, and mix it with bread crumbs, in the proportion of half a pint of suet to a quart of breadcrumbs. Moisten this with wine, season with pepper and allspice and fill the holes from which the bones were taken. Bind firmly in shape with strips of clean cloth, put in a large saucepan with part of a gravy made by boiling the trimmings of the venison; add to this a glass of port or Madeira wine and a little black pepper. Cover tightly and stew very slowly three or four hours, according to the size. It should be very tender when done. Remove the strips of cotton cloth with care, dish, and, when you have strained the gravy, pour it over the meat.

Stuffed Game Roasted

Large birds (ducks or turkeys, etc.), rabbits, hares, woodchucks, porcupines, opossums, and the like, may be stuffed with a dressing made of salt pork and bread or crackers. Chop the pork very fine, soak the bread or crackers in hot water and mash them smooth, and mix them with the chopped pork. Season with pepper, a little salt, sage and chopped onion. Sew up the game after stuffing with wire in two or three places, and roast over hot coals. If wrapped in wet brown paper it may be immersed in hot ashes and baked, if small, or may be baked the same as fish.

Woodchucks and Porcupines

When properly cooked, are little inferior to any game. They must be thoroughly parboiled before cooking, and then may be roasted or stewed. A young wood-chuck or porcupine may be baked in the ground with the hide on, after having been drawn, and is very palatable.

Opossums and Young Pigs

Are roasted alike. After cleaning the opossum or pig stuff him with bread crumbs, chopped onion and sage or summer savory for seasoning, boiled Irish and sweet potatoes (the latter especially with the 'possum) and whole boiled onions being pushed in among the dressing. Wire up the opening in two or three places, fold the legs down on the body and wire them fast. Then cut a strong, straight, hard-wood limb, and run it through the animal from stern to snout. This is to be suspended from two crotched stakes over the fire, and, if smooth, the 'possum or pig cannot be turned on it, as the limb will turn inside the animal. Therefore, in lopping off the twigs from the limb after it is cut, leave half an inch or so of each twig to act as a barb, insert the limb in the animal butt first, then give it a "yank" backward so that the barbs may hold when it is desired to turn the animal to roast all sides alike. Cut gashes in the thickest parts of the meat so that it may roast evenly throughout. A 'possum or pig prepared as above may be coated with clay and baked in the ground with plenty of coals in from two to three hours. When roasted over the fire the drippings should be caught and used to baste it.

CHAPTER V

Preparation of Vegetables for Cooking.—Time Table for Cooking Vegetables.—Cabbage, Beets, Greens, Tomatoes, Turnips, Mushrooms, Succotash, etc.

All vegetables must be carefully looked over. Remove the unripe or decayed parts, and then wash in cold water. When to be boiled they should be put in boiling salted water, and if necessary to replenish the water before the cooking is complete, boiling water should be always used. Keep the vessel covered, and drain the vegetables as soon as done. Do not let the water boil long before the vegetables are put in. Old and strong vegetables sometimes require boiling in two or three waters.

The following time table for cooking vegetables, culled from the writer's scrap-book, is reliable:

Potatoes, old, boiled, 30 minutes.

Potatoes, new, baked, 45 minutes.

Potatoes, new, boiled, 20 minutes.

Sweet potatoes, boiled, 45 minutes.

Sweet potatoes, baked, 1 hour.

Squash, boiled, 25 minutes.

Squash, baked, 45 minutes.

Shell beans, boiled, 1 hour.

Green peas, boiled, 20 to 40 minutes.

String beans, boiled, 1 to 2 hours.

Green corn, 25 minutes to 1 hour.

Asparagus, 15 to 30 minutes.

Spinach, 1 to 2 hours.

Tomatoes, fresh, 1 hour.

Tomatoes, canned, 30 minutes.[3]

Cabbage, 45 minutes to 2 hours.

Cauliflower, 1 to 2 hours.

Dandelions, 2 to 3 hours.

Beet greens, 1 hour.

Onions, 1 to 2 hours.

Beets, 1 to 5 hours.

Turnips, white, 45 minutes to 1 hour.

Turnips, yellow, 1-1/2 to 2 hours.

Parsnips, 1 to 2 hours.

Carrots, 1 to 2 hours.

---

[3] If the unopened can is put in boiling water, only about ten minutes are necessary.

If a piece of lean salt pork is boiled with some of the above, they will be sufficiently seasoned. If not, season with salt, pepper and butter.

Potatoes and Corn

For all methods of cooking these vegetables, see Chapter V. of Part I.

Boiled Cabbage

Remove the outer and all bad leaves, examining carefully for insects, and halve or quarter the cabbage, according to size. Wash, soak a short time in cold water, and put in a covered pot of boiling salted water. When it is tender and "smells good" it is done. Drain, and press out the water, seasoning with salt, pepper and butter. The latter should be omitted if it is boiled with pork.

Cabbage aux Legumes

Cut out the centre of a large cabbage, and fill the hole with small potatoes, onions, parsnips, beets, etc. Cover with a cloth and boil till tender.

Fried Cooked Cabbage

Have enough lard in the pan to just cover the bottom when melted. Chop the cabbage, put into the melted lard and stir frequently till the cabbage is piping hot, when it is ready to serve.

Succotash

Cut the corn from the cob and shell the beans. If string beans are used, string and cut into half-inch pieces. The right proportion for succotash is two-thirds corn to one-third beans. Put them into enough boiling salt water to cover them. Stew gently till tender, stirring frequently; then drain, add a cup of milk and a piece of butter the size of an egg, and stir till it boils up once. Season to taste.

Boiled Beets

Winter beets must be soaked over night in water. Wash them, but do not scrape or cut them, as they lose in color and quality by being cut. Put them in boiling water enough to cover them well, cover and boil till tender, which will take from one to three hours. Then put them in cold water and rub off the skins quickly. If large, slice them; if young, split lengthwise.

Greens

When in camp or on a cruise, a most delicious dish can be made of boiled greens, of which a large variety of weeds and plants furnishes the material. Dandelion leaves, nettles, milkweed, spinach, young beet tops, turnip tops, mustard, narrow dock, mountain cow-slip, kale, cabbage, poke, sprouts and other "weeds" are good. They should be picked over carefully, washed in three or four waters, and soaked in cold water half an hour; then drain and put in enough boiling salt water to cover them. Press them down till the pot is full, as they "boil away" and lose more than half in substance. Cover, and boil steadily till tender. Then drain and press out the water. Season to taste with butter, pepper and salt. Greens are good boiled with salt pork, bacon, corned beef or ham. Put them in the pot in time to be done with the meat.

Stewed Tomatoes

Peel by pouring over them boiling water, when the skin will easily come off. Cut up, discarding unripe and hard parts. Put into a pot, seasoning with butter, pepper, salt, and if very acid, two tablespoonfuls of sugar. Cover, and stew gently. See time table.

Boiled Turnips

Wash and peel, and if old, pare off part of the "meat" next the skin. Cut into pieces of a uniform size, soak in cold water half an hour, put into enough boiling salt water to cover them, cover, and cook according to time table. Season with butter, pepper and salt. Omit the butter if they are cooked with meat.

Mushrooms

Edible mushrooms are found in clear, open, sunny fields and elevated ground where the air is pure and fresh; poisonous ones are found in woods, low, damp ground, in shady places and upon putrefying substances. The edible kind are most plentiful in August and September, and spring up after low lying fogs, soaking dews or heavy rains. They first appear very small and of a round form, on a little stalk, the upper part and stalk being then white. They grow very fast, and, as the size increases, the under part gradually opens and shows a fringy fur (called "gills") of a delicate salmon color. After the mushroom is a day old this salmon color changes to a russet or dark brown. The gills of the poisonous variety are red, green, blue, yellow or orange red, and sometimes white, but they never have the delicate salmon color of the edible mushroom. The latter have an agreeable odor, and the poisonous have sometimes a similar odor, but generally smell fetid. The flesh of the edible kind is compact and brittle; that of the poisonous generally soft and watery. The skin of the former is easily peeled from the edges, and the seeds or sprouts are for the most part roundish or oval; the skin of the latter is not easy to peel and the seeds are mostly angular. Some poisonous ones assume a bluish tint on being bruised and others exude an acrid, milky juice. The mushroom should have all of the above-named characteristics of the edible variety before it is put in the pot, and it is safest not to select mushrooms gathered by somebody else, as they change color after being picked several hours, and the two kinds are then difficult to distinguish. Finally, if a white peeled onion cooked with them turns black, or if a silver spoon with which they are stirred while cooking turns black, don't eat them; and if you don't know a salmon color from a yellow let somebody gather them who does.

72

Stewed Mushrooms

Select mushrooms of uniform size. Wipe them clean with a soft cloth; peel, commencing at the edge and finishing at the top; cut off the lower part of the stem; put them into a tin or earthen vessel and half cover them with cold water, and stew gently for fifteen minutes, frequently stirring to prevent burning; season with pepper and salt. When the stew is done stir into it one or more tablespoonfuls of butter, previously cut in small pieces, and rolled in flour; stir three or four minutes. Do not let it boil.

Fried Mushrooms

Prepare as directed for stewing; heat in a frying pan enough butter to thinly cover the bottom; put in the mushrooms and fry both sides a golden brown.

Broiled Mushrooms

Prepare as above, put on a broiler with gills uppermost, sprinkle on a little salt and pepper and a tiny piece of butter, and hold over a bed of coals.

73

Fried Beans

Put enough butter in a frying pan to just cover the bottom when melted. When it is hot put in your beans, already boiled and drained, and fry brown, stirring occasionally.

CHAPTER VI

Boiled Rice.—Cracked Wheat.—Hominy Grits.—Batter Cakes.— Rice Cakes.—Puddings.—Welsh Rarebit.—Fried Bread for Soups.— Stewed Cranberries.

Boiled Rice

Pick one pound of rice over carefully and wash it clean in one or two cold waters, then drain and put it into a pot containing four quarts of boiling water, and add four teaspoonfuls of salt; cover and boil steadily for fifteen minutes, then drain off the water, empty the rice, wipe out the pot, sprinkle a little salt over the bottom of it and rub it with a dry cloth, finally emptying out the salt, replacing the rice and setting the pot near the fire for fifteen minutes longer to let the rice dry and swell. If a large pot is at hand a better way after the rice has boiled fifteen minutes is to drain it as above, then pouring the boiling water into the large pot, set in the dry rice in the smaller one, which should be put in the larger one and all set over the fire and the rice allowed to steam thoroughly dry, which will take fifteen minutes.

The writer followed the above recipe implicitly till he discovered that nothing further is necessary to cook rice to his own particular taste than the boiling fifteen minutes. Since making this discovery he has omitted the further portion of the recipe in practice, but gives it here for the benefit of those whose tastes may be more dainty than his own.

Cracked Wheat

To one quart of the wheat add one tablespoonful of salt, and soak over night in cold water enough to cover it. In the morning put the wheat with the water it was soaked in into a pot, cover closely and cook gently until soft—probably from one to one and one-half hours—stirring frequently to prevent scorching. When necessary to replenish the water add boiling water.

Hominy Grits

Are cooked the same as cracked wheat, and are very wholesome. Coarse hominy requires long boiling.

Batter Cakes

Put one quart of sifted flour in a deep dish, and mix with it one-half teaspoonful of salt, two heaping teaspoonfuls of baking powder and one teaspoonful of sugar. Add warm water (milk is better) sufficient to make a thick batter. Then add two eggs, beaten light, and if they do not thin down the batter sufficiently, add more water (or milk). Beat thoroughly and cook immediately the same as slapjacks.

Rice Cakes

Into one quart of sifted flour stir enough water (or milk) to make a medium thick batter; add two cups of cold boiled rice, one teaspoonful of salt, and lastly, four eggs, beaten light. Beat thoroughly and cook immediately the same as slapjacks.

Plum Pudding

Put into a basin one pound of flour, three-quarters of a pound of raisins (stoned, if possible), three-quarters of a pound of fat of salt pork (well washed and cut into small dice or chopped), and two tablespoonfuls of sugar. Add half a pint of water and mix well together. Dip a cloth bag large enough to hold the pudding into boiling water, wring it out, and apply flour well to the inside. Put in the pudding and fasten it up, leaving a little room in the bag for the pudding to swell. Now place the whole in enough boiling water to cover the bag, and boil two hours, turning the bag several times to prevent its scorching against the bottom or sides of the pot. If necessary to add water to keep the bag covered, add boiling water. When done take the pudding from the pot, plunge it into cold water for an instant, and then turn it out to be eaten.

Omaha Pudding

Mix in a deep dish one quart of sifted flour and one tablespoonful of baking powder. Dissolve one heaping teaspoonful of salt in one half pint of cold water (or milk), adding enough of the latter to the former to make a very thick batter. Mix quickly and boil in a bag as above.

Batter Pudding

One quart of sifted flour in a deep dish worked into a smooth paste with one quart of sweet milk; then mix in the yolks of seven eggs, beaten well, one teaspoonful of salt and one-fourth of a teaspoonful of baking powder dissolved in a little hot water. Stir hard and finally work in quickly the whites of the seven eggs, which should previously have been beaten into a stiff froth. Boil two hours in bags and leave plenty of room for it to swell.

Corn Starch Pudding

Dissolve three tablespoonfuls of corn starch in a small quantity of milk, add two eggs, beaten light, and a small pinch of salt. Heat three pints of milk nearly to boiling, mix all together and boil four minutes, constantly stirring. Dip a cup or basin in cold water to cool it, and turn into it the pudding, which should be eaten with sugar and milk when it is cold.

Baked Rice Pudding

Pick over and wash well one pint of rice and soak it two hours in enough milk or water to just cover it. Then stir it into two quarts of milk, one half pound of sugar, one teaspoonful of salt, and a small quantity of nutmeg or cinnamon, if at hand. Put into the baking basins, having first well greased them, and bake in the ground two or three hours till it is done brown.

Creole Sauce

The juice of a lemon, three tablespoonfuls of sugar, ditto of tomato catsup, one teaspoonful of mustard. Heat all to near the boiling point, and use hot with meats or game.

Welsh Rarebit

Cut bread into slices about one inch in thickness, and pare off the crust. Toast the slices slightly without hardening or burning and spread with butter; cut slices of cheese not quite as large as the bread, lay it on the bread, and toast all over the fire on a broiler. Be careful that the cheese does not burn, and let it be equally melted. Spread over the top a little mustard already prepared and seasoning of pepper, and serve very hot.

Fried Bread for Soups

Cut stale bread into square pieces, and fry in boiling fat for an instant. Take care it does not burn, removing it as soon as brown.

Stewed Cranberries

Pick the berries carefully; then wash them in cold water; drain. Put them into fresh cold water and allow them to remain therein five or ten minutes; drain. Then put the fruit into a well-covered pot (not iron) with sufficient boiling water to cover the berries. Stew rather quickly, stirring occasionally until soft. They should cook in from twenty to thirty minutes. Five minutes before they are done stir in sugar to taste.

CHAPTER VII

Dishes for Yachtsmen. — Macaroni, Boiled and Baked. — Baked Turkey. — Pie Crust. — Brown Betty. — Apple Pudding. — Apple Dumplings.

For the benefit of Corinthian yachtsmen, recipes are here given for some dishes which are rather too elaborate in preparation for camp purposes, but which can be cooked readily in the yacht's galley, if it be provided with a regular yacht's stove, having an oven, etc.

Boiled Macaroni

Wipe the macaroni carefully, and break it into lengths, put it into a pot of boiling salt water, say ten times as much water as macaroni. Boil fifteen to twenty minutes, or until tender. Take care that it does not burst or become a pulp from excessive boiling; drain at once and season with butter.

If desired to impart the flavor of onion to macaroni boil with it two onions for each pound of macaroni. The liquor drained from the macaroni may be used for broth or soup.

Boiled macaroni may be served with a white sauce, made as follows; for one pound of macaroni put into a pot over the fire two ounces of butter and two ounces of flour, stir until it becomes smooth, then gradually stir in one quart of hot milk and water in equal parts, season with pepper and salt, put in the macaroni, and let it remain over the fire for one minute.

Or, as soon as the butter and flour bubbles, gradually pour in one quart of boiling water, stirring it until it becomes smooth; season with pepper and salt; put in the macaroni and let it remain over the fire for one minute. Have ready one or two onions, minced or shredded, fried brown. Dish the macaroni and pour the fried onions over it.

Boiled macaroni may be served with tomato sauce made as follows: for one pound of macaroni put into a pot half a can of tomatoes, or twelve large fresh ones, one half a pint of stock, gravy, or broth of any kind, a little thyme or parsley, six whole cloves, a sliced onion, pepper and salt. Cover and boil gently for one hour, stirring frequently; drain and press the mixture through a sieve (an old pan full of nail holes will do); then stir into it about two ounces of butter and one ounce of flour, previously mixed smooth over the fire; stir until it is well incorporated; pour it over the macaroni: sprinkle on top grated cheese, and put it into the oven for five or ten minutes.

Baked Macaroni and Cheese

Boil and drain the macaroni and with it fill by layers a buttered earthen dish, seasoning each layer with butter, grated cheese, mustard, pepper, and salt; add bread crumbs for the top layer. Cover and put it into the oven, and bake with a moderate heat for a half hour. Remove the cover, and when the top is browned serve in the baking-dish.

Minced fat pork may be used instead of butter.

Baked Turkey

Tame and wild turkeys are prepared and cooked alike. The time for cooking is from fifteen to twenty minutes to the pound, but this depends much upon the age of the bird; it must be well done to be palatable. Success lies in cooking it long enough, and frequent basting.

Put the turkey into a pan of cold water; rinse it inside and out in three or four waters; in the last water but one dissolve a teaspoonful of soda. Fill the body with this water; shake it well; pour it off and rinse with fresh water; wipe it dry inside and out; rub the inside with pepper and salt. Prepare a stuffing as follows; Mix into enough grated bread crumbs to fill the craw and body of the turkey a half teaspoonful of summer savory, thyme, or sage, four ounces of lard, four ounces of butter, with enough warm water to make the mixture moist.

Mix all thoroughly and stuff the craw and body with it; tie a string tightly about the neck; sew up the incision; tie down the wings and legs; then lay it on its back in the baking-pan; wet the skin and season it with pepper and salt and dredge it with flour. Distribute on the upper side small pieces of butter; put into the pan about a pint of boiling stock or a quarter of a pound of butter; have a brisk fire; put the pan into the oven and bake. Baste frequently, at least every ten minutes; bake to a rich brown. If it browns too rapidly lay a sheet of white paper over it until the lower part is done. When the turkey is browned on the breast turn it over in the pan while in the oven.

Pepper, salt, and dredge the back with flour, and bake until browned, basting as above. When baked remove the strings from the neck and body; put it into a hot dish and serve with a flour gravy, made as described on page 60.

The turkey may also be stuffed with sausage-meat, fresh oysters or roasted chestnuts.

Pie Crust

All pie crust should be made in a cool place and handled as little as possible during the process. The heat from the hand makes the crust tough. The ingredients are:

One quart of flour (sifted); one-fourth of a pound butter; one-half teaspoonful salt; enough cold water to make a stiff dough. Sift the flour into a deep wooden bowl or tin pan; put into it the salt; mix; then the lard. With a keen chopping-knife cut up the lard into the flour until it is thoroughly incorporated, with no lumps; wet with cold water, stirring it in with a wooden spoon until it becomes a stiff dough. Flour the hands and make dough into a lump with as little handling as possible.

Remove lump to well-floured kneading-board, and roll it out into a sheet a fourth of an inch thick, always rolling from you, and with as little pressure upon the rolling-pin as may be necessary.

Into the rolled sheet stick small pieces of butter at regular intervals. Dredge slightly with flour. Roll up the sheet, commencing to roll from the side nearest you. Roll out, again buttering and dredging until the butter is exhausted. If time will permit, when the butter has been exhausted and the roll made up, lay it away in a cold place or on the ice for twenty minutes.

Place it again upon the floured kneading-board, roll out into a sheet as hereinbefore directed. Butter the pie-plates; lay the paste lightly within them, fitting it nicely. Trim off the paste neatly around the edges of the pie-plates. Gather up the cuttings and roll them into a separate sheet.

If the pies are to have a top crust, cover the tops with the paste, cutting neatly round the edges, and with a knife, spoon or the fingers join securely the edges of the top and sides to prevent escape of juices. Then with a sharp knife make three or four incisions about an inch long in the center of the top crust.

If the top crust is lightly brushed with sweet milk, it will brown evenly.

Bake in a moderate oven until a light brown. Be careful to have the heat as great at the bottom as at the top of oven. If this is not looked to, the lower crust will be uncooked and inedible.

Should a richer crust be desired the proportions of lard and butter can be doubled.

Brown Betty (Baked)

The ingredients are: Cooking-apples, pared, cored, and sliced; dry-bread crumbs, or well-toasted bread rolled into crumbs; sugar, butter, and ground cinnamon.

Grease well a deep baking-dish. Into the bottom of this put a layer of prepared apples; sprinkle them lightly with sugar; scatter small pieces of butter over this, then dust with ground cinnamon; over this place a layer of bread crumbs from one-half to three-quarters of an inch thick; over this apples, butter, and cinnamon, and continue this process until the dish is full, or until sufficient material has been used. The top layer must be crumbs, and on this must be scattered small pieces of butter. If the top layer is moistened with a couple of tablespoonfuls of milk it will brown more evenly.

Put into a moderate oven and bake from a half to three-quarters of an hour.

When a fork will easily penetrate the apples it is cooked. Alden dried apples may be substituted for the fresh fruit.

It can be eaten hot or cold with butter, sugar, or sauce.

Baked Apple Pudding

Use the following ingredients: Apples pared, cored and sliced; one quart sifted flour; three teaspoonfuls baking powder, incorporated with the dry flour; one-half teaspoonful salt; two tablespoonfuls lard (half butter is preferable); one pint milk (cold water will do).

Have ready sugar, butter, and ground cinnamon. Put flour into a deep dish or pan; mix into it the salt and lard; then add the milk, and work the mixture with the hands to a smooth light dough.

Roll the dough into a sheet about one-quarter of an inch thick. Have prepared a well-greased baking-dish. Cover the bottom and sides of the dish with rolled dough or paste, press it lightly against the sides and bottom, and cutoff the edges above the dish.

Put into the bottom of the baking-dish thus prepared a thick layer of sliced apples, sprinkle them with sugar and ground cinnamon, then another layer of apples treated in like manner, and so on successively until the dish is full. The top layer of apples should have the dressing of sugar and cinnamon, and be also sprinkled with small pieces of butter. Wet the top layer with three or four teaspoonfuls of water, and then sprinkle it lightly with dry flour.

Take the remainder of the dough, roll it out thin, and cover the dish with it, pressing the paste down round the edges of the dish to join it with the paste that lines the sides. Make three or four incisions in the cover with a sharp knife.

Then put the dish into a moderate oven and bake from one to one and a half hours. When a fork easily penetrates the pudding, it is cooked. Eat hot with sauce. Alden dried apples, canned apples, canned peaches, or fresh peaches pared, quartered, and the stones extracted may be used.

Baked Apple Dumplings

The apples pared, cored and quartered. Prepare paste as directed for Baked Apple Pudding above.

When the paste is rolled, cut it into squares, and in the centre of each square place the four parts of an apple; add to each apple a piece of butter the size of a chestnut and a small sprinkle of sugar and ground cinnamon.

Envelop the apple in the paste, pressing the cut edges together. Place the dumplings thus prepared into a well-greased baking-pan, cut edges downwards.

Bake a half to three-fourths of an hour in a moderate oven. When a fork will penetrate the dumplings they are cooked. Apples dried by the Alden process may be used.

Cooking in Iron Pots.—Let nothing stand in an iron pot after it is cooked, or it will become discolored and have an unpleasant taste.

Rusty Knives.—If knives become rusty, rub them with a fresh-cut potato dipped in ashes.

Emetic.—Gunpowder dissolved in water is a good emetic.

Save the Bacon Grease.—After frying salt pork, bacon or fat meat, do not discard the grease that is left in the pan. Keep a cup or small tin pail, in which pour all residue. It will soon harden, and is just the thing for frying slapjacks or potatoes in.

Improved River Water for Drinking.—If you make tea do not throw out the "grounds" after each drawing. In warm weather ordinary lake or river water will taste very refreshing if poured into the pot where tea-grounds have been left, and allowed to stand a few minutes before drinking.

Salt.—It is always best in cooking to use too little salt rather than too much. Further salting can be easily done at any time, but it is difficult or impossible to freshen anything that has been over-salted.

Baking Powder.—In using baking powder it is always best to follow the printed directions on the can as to the amount. The different makes of baking powders have each a different strength.

Spoons.—On a canoe trip, where storage room is at a premium, one spoon will suffice for all purposes. Let it be of iron, of "dessert" size. Get a tinsmith to cut off two inches of the handle, and solder strongly to the stump a tin cylinder one-half inch in diameter. There will be no long handle to interfere with packing it in a small space, and if a long handle is desired for skimming soups, stirring mush, etc., a stick of any length can be instantly cut to fit the tin cylinder.

Frozen Fish should be soaked in cold water to thaw them before cooking.

Fish-eating Ducks may be made palatable by parboiling them in water with an onion in it. After parboiling them throw away the onion and lay the ducks in cold water for half an hour, after which they may be roasted, broiled, fried or stewed.

Soft vs. Hard Water.—Beans, peas and other vegetables are best boiled in soft water. Hard water can be made soft (if its hardness depends upon the presence of carbonate of lime) by boiling it an hour and then allowing it to cool, when most of the lime will be precipitated.

Broiling.—Remember that it is better to broil before a fire than over it, as by the former process the juices of the meat can be caught and used as a dressing, while in the latter manner they are lost in the fire and tend to give a smoky flavor by their ignition. In broiling, the article should be turned frequently.

Frying.—The lard or fat used for frying should always be very hot before the article to be cooked is put in. If little jets of smoke issue from the top of the fat it is hot enough. If the fat is insufficiently hot, anything cooked in it will taste of the grease, while the moment a substance is dropped into fat at a great heat the exterior pores are closed, and no grease penetrates it.

Mixing Ingredients.—Preciseness in the preparation of ingredients is an important element of success in cooking. Guessing at proportions is the practice of the lazy or indifferent cook.

New Iron Pots.—Boil a handful of grass in a new iron pot, then scrub it inside with soap and sand, fill it with clean water and let this boil half an hour. It is then ready to use for cooking.

Table of Approximate Weights and Measures.—The following table may be of use. It is near enough to accuracy for cooking purposes:—

Three teaspoonfuls = One tablespoonful.

Four tablespoonfuls = One wine glass.

Two wine glasses = One gill.

Two gills = One tumbler or cup.

Two cupfuls = One pint.

One quart sifted flour = One pound.

One quart powdered sugar = One pound, seven ounces.

One quart granulated sugar = One pound, nine ounces.

One pint closely packed butter = One pound.

Three cupfuls sugar = One pound.

Five cupfuls sifted flour = One pound.

One tablespoonful salt = One ounce.

Seven tablespoonfuls granulated sugar = One half pint.

Twelve tablespoonfuls flour = One pint.

Three coffee cupfuls = One quart.

Ten eggs = One pound.

Yeast.—A serviceable yeast for leavening bread may be made by mixing flour and cold water into a thin batter. Set it away in a bottle until it sours, when it is ready for use.

CPSIA information can be obtained
at www.ICGtesting.com
Printed in the USA
BVHW071202270123
657291BV00007B/1567